R & D MYTH OR MAGIC?

Nine MythsThat Can Seriously Damage Your

Wealth

by

Keith Trubshaw

Research & Development
R & D Myth or Magic?
Nine Myths That Can Seriously Damage Your Wealth.

Author: Keith Trubshaw
e.mail: mythormagic@therefund.agency
Please direct all enquiries to the author

© 2019 All rights reserved

Disclaimer

The contents of this book have been created as a result of a combination of extensive examination of legislation-based texts and the experience of presentating many reports to HMRC, all of which have resulted in successful claims. However the book is meant as a humerous layman's guide and its contents are not be relied upon in the formulation and presentation of Research & Development claims.

CONTENTS

i	Introduction.	5
ii	Research & Development; Two words but what do they mean?	8
iii	What are they?	10
iv	The Nine Myths.	11
1	It's all about men in white coats.	12
2	A Project has to have been successful.	15
3	My Accountant deals with this	17
4	Our claim wouldn't be worth doing.	22
5	Claiming will result in a Tax Investigation	24
6	We Don't do R & D.	28
7	Can't claim because we don't pay Tax.	30
8	We Don't have Time.	32
9	We have Plenty of Time	33
v	Image Credits	34
vi	About the Author	35

INTRODUCTION

Hello. How many books on business are we offered during the course of a year? Chances are that many of us are inundated; read this; follow that guru; how to make a million in the blink of an eye. If it were that easy then we would all be multi millionaires. Indeed if business was easy, everyone would have one. Business is not easy. Okay maybe sometimes it is; those are the good days; the diamond days, and if we're lucky they outnumber the bad. In general though, much like life, business is a rollercoaster of good times and bad times, with successes and failures littered all along the track.

The average managing director strives to make their business successful by improving in whatever way they can. Sales levels maximized, the methods by which it produces its widgets streamlined to be as efficient as possible, the list goes on. So many have often said that all they ask for is a level playing field. It's sad that the majority don't realise that there's help out there to achieve just that, sadder still is that of those who know such help exists, too many simply ignore it; too busy chasing the next contract, that sale which is the very essence of why they got into business in the first place.

In all of my years in business there was one thing that I failed to learn. Scrub that! There were thousands of things that I failed to learn, but one of the most important was this:

I was always too busy chasing the next sale; too busy firefighting; dealing with issues of survival to open my eyes and ears to what was out there which could have helped my company.

Consider this; if the overheads are such that a company's net profit on sales is around 5% (and that's as good as it gets for some companies) then a £10,000 sale adds £500 to the bottom line at the end of the year. That sale may well have taken months of preparation and effort before the client finally signed on the dotted line and yet the effort was considered worthwhile. Perhaps worse, in many businesses it was the Managing Director who did all of the work to get the order; while they were engaged in the process they had no time to listen to anything offered to them which might have diverted their attention from that task. And yet effectively locked within the business for the want of a conversation is ten, twenty, maybe thirty thousand pounds or more of pure bottom line profit which would, with the right help, take just a few hours to unlock before appearing in the bank just a few weeks later. Make no mistake, such figures are very real. I have worked on instances where the money that arrives in the bank account has saved a business from closure.

This money is in the form of Research and Development Tax Credits paid by HMRC to companies who have taken time and trouble to do things better; to make things work; to come up with solutions for what were often to them, everyday problems; problems that they'd had to solve anyhow.

RESEARCH & DEVELOPMENT;
TWO WORDS BUT WHAT DO THEY MEAN?

The Oxford English Dictionary defines Research as:

"The systematic investigation into and study of materials and sources in order to establish facts and reach new conclusions."

In the business environment how much time is spent in seeking new and better ways of doing things, striving to find better forms of materials, or buying rival products just to take them apart so as to try to make a better one.

It's a fact that more R & D is paid out in respect of "Development" than is paid out for "Research".

The Oxford English Dictionary's definition of the noun that is "Development" leaves us in no doubt as to why this is so. (Noun): Development: *A specified state of growth or advancement.*

If a business does not develop either itself or its products, then its downfall is a matter of time.

(Verb): Develop: *Grow or cause to grow and become more mature, advanced, or elaborate.*

There is little to add here. Who am I to presume that I can add to the eloquence of the Oxford English Dictionary. I would simply suggest that if you are sure that your company does not engage in R & D re-read those definitions. If, after doing so, you are still sure that you don't indulge in such practices, close the book and give it to someone that you want to see do well.

WHAT ARE THEY?

Research and Development Tax credits have been around since 2002. They are the government's way of rewarding businesses for innovation; for making British Business the best it can be. I first came across R & D Funding in 2008 and was enthralled at the possibilities, lamenting that I had known nothing about it in my days in engineering which had come to an abrupt end in 2007. I secured my first grant when consulting for a pneumatics company in 2012. In doing so I used the services of specialist, without whom the claim would not have succeeded. Research and Development funding is available to limited companies, not individuals or partnerships as it is part of the UKs corporation tax strategy. Too often I am asked by sole traders, who are nothing less than geniuses at what they do, if I can help them. Unfair as it may seem I have to say no. But for limited companies this can be a Pandora's Box full of rewards they never dreamed of. That is not to say that the system is there to be abused, if you wish to abuse it then it is a matter of some regret to me that this book is in your hands, for in abusing it you will speed the withdrawal of what is a wonderful piece of legislation.

THE NINE MYTHS.

In all the years of my helping clients there are common themes as to why businesses fail to take advantage of what is rightfully theirs. It is no accident that I have maintained a light hearted view as I describe them; If I didn't laugh I would cry at the millions (yes millions) that goes begging every year at the hands of bad advice or no advice at all.

> *"We are sitting on a whole pile of money which we are tasked to give away, but no one comes for it because they either don't know it exists or if they do, they don't know how to claim it properly".* HMRC's R & D application review senior team staff member.

MYTH NUMBER ONE.

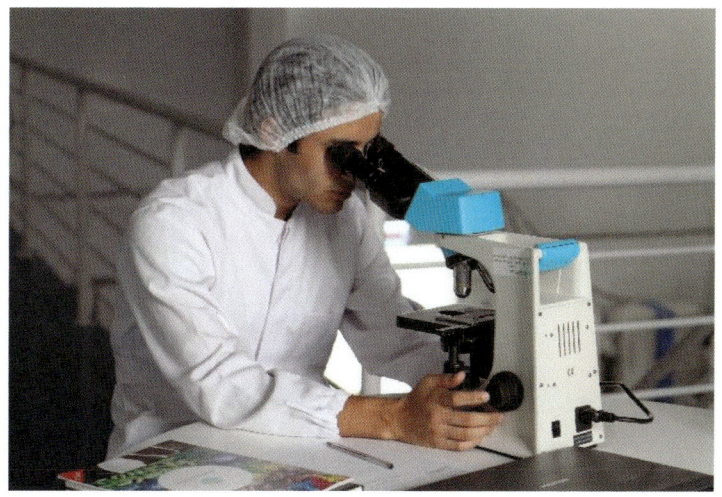

IT'S ALL ABOUT MEN IN WHITE COATS.

What percentage of British companies employ men in white coats? What percentage of British companies employ women in white coats? The answer to both questions is, I would suggest, very few. White coats are synonymous with laboratories; lines of people dealing with substances with complicated names and speaking in a curious language which consists almost exclusively of chemical formulae. This is the perception that so many companies have of what research and development looks like.

That perception is not wrong; very often a laboratory is indeed a place where research and development takes place, but it is by no means the only place.

<u>Trial and Error</u>

Consider the engineering company who is trying to produce a component that will not keep breaking down under load. They keep trying until they succeed. This is the very essence of R & D. The trial and error they have undertaken has taken time and resources, with no guarantee of success.

Or what about the company that takes on the task of connecting two pieces of a very specific kind of plastic. Using screws or any other form of metal fastener is not an option, so they have to use adhesive. The trouble is that there is no recommendation within the industry as to what kind of adhesive will successfully glue that kind of plastic.

Time after time they carry out trials only for them to fail. It is only after many weeks that they finally come up with a solution that works. There was no text book or expert they mighthave consulted, they'd had to find the answer for themselves. The cost of all of that trial and error, the employees' time, the materials thrown into the bin when they failed' was all legitimate R & D.

So, it's simply not about people in white coats. Thousands of companies constantly undertake R & D just by tackling the problems they face every day.

MYTH NUMBER TWO.

A PROJECT HAS TO HAVE BEEN SUCCESSFUL

Not every project succeeds. History tells us that the Industrial revolution would never have happened if the only projects undertaken were the ones guaranteed to succeed. The steam engine would not have got off the drawing board. Many engineers gained fame and fortune as it was developed and in the days before health and safety legislation many people died as pressure vessels exploded before James Watt revolutionized its use in the second half of the eighteenth century.

By now I know that I am stating the obvious, but all those efforts; all of that pioneering work; **was R & D.**

That discarded machine in the corner that didn't quite work; the one you will eventually get around to when you get the time; could well be the source of your next R & D payment. That software you played around with but eventually set aside because you couldn't get it to do what you wanted; that too was **R & D.**

If at first you don't succeed.

HMRC recognise the fact that not every attempt to improve things succeeds. The legislation was written to reward those who *try!* That way, they will be prepared to try again.

MYTH NUMBER THREE.

MY ACCOUNTANT DEALS WITH THIS.

I will come down off the fence here (not that I was ever on it in the first place). This old chestnut is my favourite, I hear different versions of those words every day. A business owner's relationship with their accountant is very often closer than it is with their spouse. They hang on every word that the accountant utters, but saddest of all, too many accountants start to believe that misconception so prevalent amongst their clients to be fact. They pronounce on all sorts of topics to an extent that a lawyer would never dream of. Lawyers understand that every area of law requires a different area of specialization. When they are asked for advice on a legal matter outside their area of expertise (and insurance cover for that matter) they simply inform their would-be client of that fact and pass them to another lawyer who they know to be expert in that particular field. Too many accountants do not recognise that there are myriad areas of specialty; their stock answer when faced with a client who wants advice on something outside the accountant's area of expertise is "No. Don't do it". I am not saying that all accountants behave this way, but too many do. How can you be sure that your accountant is not one of those?

All too often I hear the words "Oh my accountant is brilliant". In these circumstances, my question is always the same; "How do you know? What measure have you used to assess them?" I have played guitar for forty years, my brother, bless him described me once or twice as a "great guitarist!" How could he know? He doesn't play guitar so has no stick to measure me by. My musician friends know only too well that compared to some of them I am barely competent. Of course, what I am writing about applies to everyone we might hold in high regard; doctors; teachers; business gurus. Just because they tell us they're good is no guarantee that they actually *are!* And it's a certainty that they won't know everything about everything. If you happen to *be* an accountant, my appeal to you is this… if you are an expert in a particular piece of legislation, by all means sing it from the tree tops, but when you're not; when you know that your understanding falls some way short of "expert", do what doctors do; refer the patient to an expert. That way you are doing right by your client, and reducing the possibility of being sued at some point in the future when your client finally realises what they *could* have had.

Let me give you a real example. Not too long ago I carried out a forensic analysis of the activities of a company that revealed a potential claim of some £20,000. All that was needed to complete the claim were copies of the previous two years' tax returns from their accountant (see picture at the head of this chapter), their response was something along the lines of. "We have looked at your books and we only think your claim is worth about £2000 and we will only charge you 10% to get it for you". The accountant declined my offer to meet.

Two questions arise here which the client should perhaps have asked;

- Have you interviewed us as to what we did when creating our invention?
- If you're sure it should have been £2000 why didn't you claim it on the tax return that you charged us for doing?

Okay, I can't resist, let me cite another very real case.

A small telecom client was persuaded to let my company take a second look at what their accountant had submitted for them as far as their R & D was concerned. We looked at what had been put through then interviewed the client, going through everything they had done which we could identify as legitimate R & D. We identified some £68,000 of legitimate spending. The accountant had shown the princely sum of £500 which they had "estimated" to be the correct amount. It is not just my company;*The Refund Agency* which has such horror stories. Experts all over the country can repeat countless similar tales. In this case the outcome was highly successful, but if the client had not consulted with a specialist, the money would have been lost forever and they would never have known.

There are lawyers who make a very nice living from pursuing the providers of bad advice. But we love and respect our accountants so much we don't take up such services. But do they all deserve such love and respect I wonder?

> **Note:** *Just because a claim has been made, there is nothing to prevent you from re-visiting that claim provided that it has not been timed out under HMRC rules*

MYTH NUMBER FOUR.

OUR CLAIM WOULDN'T BE WORTH DOING.

Throughout most of this book, what I have written about how specialist consultants can help make the most of a legitimate R & D claim goes for all of the honest and properly insured R & D consultants around the country. It is not the case here however. There are many excellent consultants who in certain circumstances will not entertain doing the work necessary to enter a claim with HMRC. Almost all work on a success fee and if that fee is too low they will simply walk away. I know of consultants who will turn their nose up at cases if they think they will be less than £100,000 I do not subscribe to that view, I believe that today's acorn is tomorrow's oak tree, and frankly gain just as much if not more pleasure securing a few hundred pounds for a tiny one man band as I get from securing six figures for a larger company.

The thing is, no matter how small the claim. It is possible to get it done. The money is rightfully yours and nothing should prevent that.

MYTH NUMBER FIVE.

CLAIMING WILL RESULT IN A TAX INVESTIGATION.

This book is about showing things to be myth and they don't come any bigger than this. We all know that people in glass houses shouldn't throw stones. If you were HMRC would you not wonder, why a company that clearly carries out R & D has never made a claim. There is no evidence that I am aware of that any claim I have been involved with has ever precipitated an HMRC investigation.

Those are my words, but I would suspect that every R & D consulting firm in the UK would say the same.

That's not to say that it can't happen. If you blatantly tell lies and make a fraudulent claim, then you run the risk of being caught and punished in the same way as if you tell lies on your tax return. For our part *The Refund Agency* will not be party to fraudulent claims. If we suspect that our clients are being less than honest we will not process their claim. Doubtless there are those out there somewhere who will, but to me this is free money. Why abuse it?

MYTH NUMBER SIX.

WE DON'T DO R & D.

Who told you that? Hopefully not your accountant, if it was, then I would refer you to the previous chapter. In my experience, an experience shared I suspect by many other R & D specialists across the country, companies are simply not aware that so much of their solving what to them, are every-day problems and challenges constitutes R & D. It is worth pointing out that more is paid out for development than for research, but when we examine that fact it is perhaps easy to see why. So many companies have to adapt and re-adapt ideas, concepts and machinery to make them fit the job in hand. So many companies stretch themselves financially to buy a piece of machinery or software in the belief that it will help them solve a particular issue, only to find that it does not quite do so. So, with their finite resources, what choice do they have but to spend often countless hours trying to make it work.

How many times have we said "yes" when a client calls, only to put down the phone wondering how the heck we we're going perform the miracle required by what we have just said "yes" to. I am not saying for one moment that all of those instances constitute legitimate R & D, but the thing is; many of them do!

MYTH NUMBER SEVEN.

WE CAN'T CLAIM BECAUSE WE DON'T PAY CORPORATION TAX.

This is the easiest myth easiest to deal with. The legislation is clear.

A company does not have to have ever paid Corporation Tax to be able to successfully claim Research and Development Tax Credits.

The Government recognizes that there are countless companies, who have still to reach profitability, yet nevertheless put huge resources into Research and Development. Those companies can elect to have a tax- credit set against future profits or (and most do) take a cash settlement calculated at a slightly lower rate than the full credit. This cash injection can breathe new life into a company as it strives to grow, and quite frankly can be the difference between success and failure.

MYTH NUMBER EIGHT.

WE DON'T HAVE TIME.

In fairness this isn't so much of a myth as an area where so many get their priorities out of balance. Time and time again I meet company directors who are incredibly busy and often stressed to high heaven. They work non-stop; morning till night and by the time they eventually get home they collapse in front of the TV. My very much non-scientific research indicates that it is not always the pursuit of profit (or worse still, turnover) that drives these people, it is the fact that they are pursuing the reason why they are in business; they make widgets or service widgets, it's simply who they are. Ask them to take time out to sit for hours on end to complete the necessary documentation for an R & D claim and we have more chance of getting them to fly to the moon. But the thing is, it doesn't have to be that way. That's why specialist consultants exist. You may now be thinking that this is simply a plea for work. If so then I'm sorry to disappoint you because this is a plea for common sense. Use a consultant and a few minutes of your time has the potential to deliver extraordinary benefits. Think of it this way; if you can make time for a cup of coffee, then chances are in the time it takes to drink it, you could have had a conversation to start the ball rolling on your R & D claim. I am not going to claim that is all the time it will take, because that wouldn't be true. Depending on how much you can delegate it might take you a few hours over a period of a few weeks. However, the rewards are usually exponential. Finally, consider this: many businesses owe their success to the Managing Director's ability to keep their nose to the grind-stone; but sadly, many owe their failure to exactly the same scenario; noses applied to grind-stones mean that we cannot look up and spot other opportunities; they just sail by us.

MYTH NUMBER NINE.

WE HAVE PLENTY OF TIME.

If you take nothing else from this short book, take away the knowledge that there is a good chance that despite what you may think, your company *does* have the basis for a claim for R & D tax credits. Depending where you are in your financial year you can go

~~back up to two years when making a claim, but not a day longer.~~ As your year-end ticks over into a new one, then any claim you may have had in respect of the year that ended 24 months ago will be lost.

So, the message is clear. Do not leave money that is legitimately yours on the table. Claim it NOW before it's too late. The process is not complicated if you take the right advice. And the rewards can be surprisingly substantial.

THANKS FOR READING

Image Credits

Cover: Osman Rana on Unsplash

"If at first you don't succeed": Christian Sterk on Unsplash

Myth Images:

1. Lucas Vasques on Unsplash
2. Clever Visuals on Unsplash
3. Licenced from Getty images
4. Licenced from Getty Images
5. Licenced from Getty Images
6. Licenced from Getty Images
7. Courtesy of HMRC
8. Elena Koycheva on Unsplash
9. Neonbrand on Unsplash

ABOUT THE AUTHOR

Along with his Business Partner; Bob Boardman, Keith Trubshaw is a director of The Refund Agency which specializes in securing Research & Development tax credits. His three decades at the sharp-end of business together with his education in accountancy and law combines well with his creative writing skills when working on this book and behalf of clients across the UK. He is a musician, author, poet, and more recently, a playwright and public speaker. He can be contacted by emailing…

mythormagic@therefund.agency

Printed in Great Britain
by Amazon